In
CLASSICAL
mood

Musical Travels

Musical Travels

Take an armchair journey to the far corners of the globe with this volume of *In Classical Mood* and experience the ways in which travel has inspired great composers. Capturing the vibrant spirit of the New World are pieces by Gershwin, Milhaud, and Villa-Lobos, while Debussy and the little-known Chinese composer Wang Xi Lin explore the delicacy and mystery of the Orient. On a slightly different note, Honegger's *Pacific 231* and Ravel's *Miroirs* evoke stirring images of journeys by land and sea, and Rossini paints a typically lively picture of a journey to the French town of Reims. *Musical Travels* is as varied and full of surprises as the world itself and presents much listening pleasure.

THE LISTENER'S GUIDE — WHAT THE SYMBOLS MEAN

THE COMPOSERS
Their lives... their loves.. their legacies...

THE MUSIC
Explanation... analysis... interpretation...

THE INSPIRATION
How works of genius came to be written

THE BACKGROUND
People, places, and events linked to the music

Contents

WOLFGANG AMADEUS MOZART *1756–1791*

Piano Sonata in A Major

K331: THIRD MOVEMENT (RONDO ALLA TURCA)

This "Turkish Rondo" has the air of a quick and swaggering march. The piece has a main theme which keeps coming around again, true to rondo form, and is punctuated by other equally bright tunes. Although this is a movement from a piano sonata, Mozart cleverly manages to suggest the percussion of a traditional Turkish Janissary band and to infuse the music with a hint of Oriental melody and rhythm. Musical hybrids such as this give us a glimpse of how remote and exotic the Near and Middle East appeared to people in 18th-century Europe, when travel was restricted to the adventurous few.

THE OTTOMAN EMPIRE

Mozart's "Turkish Rondo" reflects the craze for everything Turkish that was sweeping Vienna at the time he wrote it, in the early 1780s. The Ottoman, or Turkish, empire

dates back to around 1300. Its greatest triumph was the capture, in 1453, of the old Christian Byzantine capital

Constantinople *(above)*, now known as Istanbul. During the next two centuries, the Turks advanced across southern and eastern Europe until they were within one hundred miles of Vienna. By Mozart's lifetime, the threat from the Turks had passed, and their empire had fallen into decline.

Left: *"The Magnificent" Suleiman ruled the Ottoman Empire for forty-six years in the 16th century.*

JANISSARY BANDS

In his "Turkish Rondo," Mozart imitates the style of the Janissary bands. The Janissaries *(below)* were the sultan's bodyguards. Their bands consisted mainly of percussion instruments such as drums, cymbals, and triangles. Another instrument they played was the "Jingling Johnny" or "Turkish Crescent"—a long pole with one or more crescent-shaped arms to which small bells are attached. Shaking the pole produces an effect similar to sleigh bells.

KEY NOTES

Mozart also wrote an opera on a Turkish theme, Die Entführung aus dem Serail ("The Abduction from the Harem"). This, too, brings in the music of a Janissary band.

MAURICE RAVEL
1875–1937

Miroirs

UNE BARQUE SUR L'OCÉAN

In this orchestral version of Ravel's charming piano piece, a languorous theme on the woodwind suggests the *barque* or packet boat (a passenger boat carrying cargo and mail), while accompanying strings call to mind images of a sea breeze and shimmering light on water. As the music proceeds, there are other impressions—of a stiffening wind, waves, and spray—but the overall mood remains one of a hazy summer day. The music comes to an end as the boat finally disappears from sight over the rim of the horizon to the soft, delicate chimes of the celesta.

FROM PIANO TO ORCHESTRA

"Une Barque sur l'océan" ("A Boat on the Ocean") is part of a group of five piano pieces by Maurice Ravel collectively entitled *Miroirs* (*"Mirrors"*). The other four are: "Noctuelles" ("Night Creatures"), "Oiseaux tristes" ("Sad Birds"), "Alborada del gracioso" ("Morning Song of the Jester"), and "La Vallée des cloches" ("The Valley of Bells").

CONSOLATION PRIZE

Ravel's *Miroirs* in 1905 coincided with his failure to win, on his fourth attempt, the Paris Conservatoire de Musique's most coveted music award, the Prix de Rome. The injustice of his loss created a public outcry, as other leading French

musicians and intellectuals condemned the jury of the Conservatoire for their prejudice and shortsightedness, while praising Ravel *(right)* as the rising new star of French music. As a result, the director of the Conservatoire, Théodore Dubois *(caricatured left)*, was forced to resign. Ravel may have failed to win the Prix de Rome, but the resulting publicity did him no harm at all!

RECORD BREAKERS

When Ravel wrote "Une Barque sur l'océan" in 1905, the great days of the ocean liner had begun. There was the excitement of the "Blue Riband" awarded to the ship that made the fastest Atlantic crossing. The rivalry was intense. In 1907, the *Lusitania* won the prize for Britain. The *Mauretania (right)*, also a Cunard liner, seized the record in 1909 and kept it for an amazing twenty years, until beaten by Germany's *Bremen* in 1929. The *Queen Mary* and France's *Normandie* followed. The last winner was the *United States*, in 1952.

KEY NOTES

In 1905, after failing to win the Prix de Rome, Ravel set off on his own boat trip. Invited to join his friends on their yacht, Aimée, he delighted in seeing new sights. "I am storing it all away," he wrote, "and think many things will come from this cruise."

DARIUS MILHAUD *1892–1974*

Le Boeuf sur le toit

OPUS 58: EXCERPT

Written in the wake of Milhaud's trip to Brazil in 1917, *Le Boeuf sur le toit* (*"The Ox on the Roof"*) is from a Brazilian song, and the music transports the listener to carnival time in Rio. The piece is basically in rondo form with the opening theme recurring, with other episodes introduced in between. The rhythm of the Brazilian samba and other Latin American dances, combined with the tunes of popular songs, builds up to a heady climax. This excerpt contains several striking examples of polytonality (music played in several different keys at the same time)—a favorite device of Milhaud's.

AMERICAN INFLUENCES

Darius Milhaud *(below right)* was born in 1892 in the southern French town of Aix-en-Provence. Already writing music at the age of seven, he studied at the Paris Conservatoire de Musique, where one of his teachers was Paul Dukas (composer of *The Sorcerer's Apprentice*). At the outbreak of World War I, Milhaud was rejected for military service and decided to travel to Brazil, where he fell in love with Latin American music. On his return, he joined the group of young French composers known as "Les Six." But he was soon traveling again, this time visiting New York *(above)*, where jazz greatly impressed him. In 1940, forced to flee German-occupied France because he was a Jew, he returned to the U.S., where he taught music. Although crippled with arthritis, he continued traveling and writing copious amounts of music well into his seventies. He died in Geneva in 1974.

BALLET BY JEAN COCTEAU

Milhaud originally felt that the music to *Le Boeuf sur le toit* might be suitable to accompany a Charlie Chaplin silent movie. It was, in fact, first performed in Paris in 1920 as a kind of music hall entertainment. Later, the celebrated writer and designer Jean Cocteau *(left)*, a close friend of Milhaud and "Les Six," turned the music into a ballet. This was set in a bar, or "speakeasy," during the period of prohibition in the U.S. and featured characters born from Cocteau's typically whimsical imagination.

SOUTH AMERICAN RHYTHMS

The intoxicating rhythms of Latin America (South and Central America and the Caribbean) come from a mixture of ancient tribal dances, the chants of African slaves, and the popular songs and dances of the Spanish and Portuguese, who colonized the vast region. One of the most famous of all Latin American dances is the sultry *tango*, which originated in Argentina and was for a long time frowned upon in respectable society as being too "suggestive." The more lively *samba (left)* and the relaxed and languid *bossa nova* come from nearby Brazil. The energetic *rumba* and the big band *salsa* belong to the island of Cuba.

JAZZED UP

The syncopated, off-beat rhythms of Latin American music and jazz have much in common, and Milhaud loved them both. A visit in 1922 to clubs in Harlem, New York *(right)*, exposed him to the classic jazz harmonies of the blues and the jaunty beat of "stomps" and "rags." His visit also inspired another of his best-known works, *La Création du monde* (*"The Creation of the World"*), a ballet based on African-American legends that was one of the first pieces to bring jazz into the concert hall.

KEY NOTES

For a long time, Milhaud was regarded as an avant-garde composer because of such works as Machines agricoles—*a group of songs based on the topic of farm machinery!*

GIOACHINO ROSSINI *1792–1868*

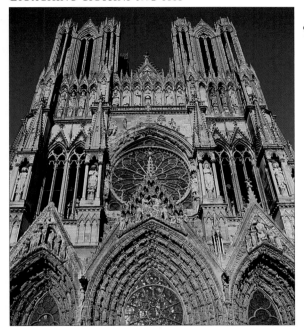

Il Viaggio a Reims

OVERTURE

In 1825, Rossini was asked by King Charles X of France to write a work celebrating his coronation in the cathedral of Reims. Rossini obliged with *Il Viaggio a Reims* (*"The Journey to Reims"*). The piece opens grandly, then gives way to a graceful melody, which is first heard on a solo oboe. The main section enters with violins leading to a crescendo that only Rossini could write.

ROYAL CITY

Since the crowning of Clovis as King of the Franks in A.D. 481, Reims has seen the coronation of nearly every French monarch. The cathedral was completed in time for the 1429 crowning of Charles VII, at which Joan of Arc was present.

KEY NOTES

In 1825, Rossini was appointed Charles X's official composer, with a lucrative contract for new operas. But the unpopular Charles was deposed by the revolution of 1830, and Rossini's contract was set aside. Rossini took the matter to court and won a pension from the new French government.

HEITOR VILLA-LOBOS *1887–1959*

A Lenda do Caboclo

A Lenda do Caboclo means "Tales of the Caboclo," and refers to a Brazilian people of mixed European and Native American descent. The piece expresses the composer's love for the rich musical and cultural heritage of his homeland, with its European and American roots. Originally for piano, its haunting melody is given extra color in this arrangement for classical guitars. Some passages may also suggest the harp, an instrument popular in many parts of South America. The overall impression is of the drowsy heat of Brazil, stretching inland from the coast, across the plateau, to the dense rain forests of the Amazon and its tributaries.

A BRAZILIAN HERO

Heitor Villa-Lobos *(right)* is Latin America's most celebrated composer. He was born in Rio de Janeiro *(below)* in 1887 and had his first music lessons from his father, who taught him to play the cello. Beyond that, his musical education came from traveling around South America, listening to

local musicians while forming his own musical style. Success came slowly, and Villa-Lobos was well over thirty before his music gained any acclaim. He wrote *A Lenda do Caboclo* in 1920. Three years later he left for Paris, where his talent was at last fully recognized, and he returned to Brazil in 1930 as something close to a national hero. Official appointments followed, but he went on composing and produced one of the largest bodies of music of any 20th-century composer. Villa-Lobos died in 1959, having put Brazil on the world's musical map.

SOUTH AMERICAN GIANT

Brazil is by far the largest country in South America. Pedro Álvares Cabral secured the territory of Brazil for Portugal in 1500. The European settlers who followed killed many of the Native Americans and imported African slaves to work the land. By 1800, well over half the population was of African origin. Slavery was not abolished until 1888.

BRAZILIAN MUSIC

Its mixture of races and regions has endowed Brazil with a rich musical heritage. In the depths of the Amazon rain forest, the Native Americans *(right)* still use such primitive instruments as the bull-roarer—a slice of wood which is whirled around in the air on a length of cord, creating a whistling, rushing sound. The songs and dances of the Portuguese settlers have given rise to the local traditions of the *toados*, or love songs, and the *chôro*, or folk

music bands (inspiring an important group of works by Villa-Lobos called *Chôros*). And, of course, there are the seductive Latin American rhythms of the samba and the lazy bossa nova (made famous by the song "The Girl from Ipanema"). It was this vast array of influences that Villa-Lobos blended so cleverly into an extraordinary output of over 3,000 works.

ROYAL COMMISSION

In 1922 the Belgian King Albert and Queen Elisabeth *(left)* visited Brazil, and Villa-Lobos was asked to write a symphony in their honor. He called it *A Guerra* (*"To War"*), referring to World War I when Germany invaded Belgium. He conducted the work at a gala concert, which also celebrated one hundred years of Brazilian independence. It proved to be the turning point of his career.

KEY NOTES

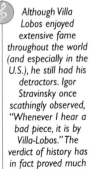

Although Villa Lobos enjoyed extensive fame throughout the world (and especially in the U.S.), he still had his detractors. Igor Stravinsky once scathingly observed, "Whenever I hear a bad piece, it is by Villa-Lobos." The verdict of history has in fact proved much less harsh.

CAMILLE SAINT-SAËNS
1835–1921

Africa

FANTASY FOR PIANO AND ORCHESTRA, OPUS 89

Following the death of his mother in 1888, Saint-Saëns increasingly began to indulge his passion for foreign travel. It was during a visit to the Canary Islands, just off the North African coast, that he started to sketch this colorful fantasy. The opening passages—including a virtuoso part for piano—owe a debt to late-19th-century European music. But the true African influences of the piece emerge in the concluding part, where Saint-Saëns introduces a traditional Tunisian folk melody into this jolly scherzo.

PIANO PRODIGY

Saint-Saëns's astonishing gifts as a pianist are sometimes overlooked. At the age of four he could play the piano part in one of Beethoven's sonatas for violin and piano. By the time he was five, he was composing his own little piano pieces. Another five years later he was playing Beethoven's piano concertos in public.

KEY NOTES

Saint-Saëns's love for travel is reflected in his works. Besides *Africa*, he wrote an Algerian suite called *Arabian caprices*, a piano concerto nicknamed the *Egyptian*, and songs about Persia.

ARTHUR HONEGGER
1892–1955

Pacific 231

MOUVEMENT SYMPHONIQUE NO.1

he title *Pacific 231* refers to the mighty Pacific-class steam locomotives that enjoyed their heyday in the mid-20th century (the number *231* indicates the wheel grouping on the engine). Honegger, who loved trains, wanted to convey the sense of power and motion a large steam locomotive at the head of an express train has as it starts up, gathers speed, and races through the countryside. The hiss of steam, the percussive snorts of the exhaust, and the accelerating motion of wheels, rods, and pistons are all reproduced—mainly by the brass and percussion. The piece remains one of the most graphic and thrilling evocations of mechanical power ever captured in music.

A SWISS FRENCHMAN

Although he maintained Swiss nationality throughout his life, Arthur Honegger was born in the French port of Le Havre *(below)*, in 1892. He studied at the Paris Conservatoire de Musique before joining the group of French composers known as "Les Six." *Pacific 231*, dating from 1923, made him famous. But his serious frame of mind soon distanced him from the more playful

spirit of "Les Six." He wrote five symphonies, and, in 1935, what is now regarded as his masterpiece, the oratorio *Jeanne d'Arc au bûcher* ("Joan of Arc at the Stake"). During World War II, Honegger remained in Paris teaching and also working for the Resistance. He was touring the U.S. when he fell ill with heart disease, and died in his Paris apartment in 1955.

Honegger (above, right) *in front of a Pacific-class locomotive.*

ALL STEAMED UP

The 1920s and 1930s were the golden age of train travel, as railroad companies rivaled each other in terms of speed and comfort. Two of the most glamorous trains of the time started from Paris: the Orient Express, which traveled all the way to Istanbul; and the Blue Train, an overnight express to the French Riviera. The United States's most luxurious train of the period was the Twentieth Century Limited.

KEY NOTES

Pacific 231 *is the first of three "symphonic movements." The second is* Rugby, *inspired by the game, and the third is sometimes called* Summer Pastoral.

PERCY GRAINGER *1882–1961*

Sentimentals

COLONIAL SONG

Australian-born Percy Grainger was living in Europe when he wrote "Colonial Song," in its piano version, in 1911. It shows that while he was very much a part of European society, and the friend of such eminent composers as Grieg and Delius, he retained fond memories of his distant homeland. The music expresses both pride and nostalgia, taking on the character of a national anthem. At one time, Grainger expressed hope that this piece might actually be adopted as Australia's national song.

SENTIMENTALS: COLONIAL SONG

AUSTRALIA'S HISTORY

Australia takes its name from the Latin *terra australis*, or "The Southern Land." While the Aborigines from southeast Asia are thought to have been the first inhabitants of Australia some 40,000 years ago, one of the first European explorers to reach it was the Dutchman Abel Tasman, in 1642 (after whom

Tasmania is named). In 1770, Englishman Captain James Cook claimed the eastern coast for Britain. For many years it was used as a penal colony for convicts, but by the time of Grainger's birth in 1882, Australia was beginning to acquire a sense of national identity.

Above: *Captain Cook claims New South Wales for Britain.*
Left: *The Devil's Marbles in the heart of Australia's arid outback.*

ANGLO-SAXON MAN

Once in Europe, the eccentric Grainger *(right)* invented his own vocabulary to avoid words of non-Anglo-Saxon origin. Music became "tone-art," a restaurant was "an eat-shop," and religion was "God-belief." His views on music were almost as strange. He considered much European music to be fussy, equating it with an overcultivated countryside of hills, rivers, woods, and fields. He believed that Australia's desert landscape should inspire a new kind of music, free from such "restrictions."

KEY NOTES

The famous conductor Thomas Beecham once told Grainger to his face that "Colonial Song" was one of the worst pieces of music ever written. Yet this didn't deter Beecham from including it in many of his concerts over the years.

WANG XI LIN

𝒴unnan 𝒮cenes

SPRING RAINFALL AT THE TEA FARM

Though set in the heart of China, this piece was deliberately written for a Western-style symphony orchestra. It also uses a number of intriguing instrumental effects—from the soft opening phrases on woodwind over gently rippling strings and harp arpeggios, to the rhapsodic main theme, played on soaring violins. Taken as a whole, the music paints a colorful picture of a subtropical land of dramatic contrasts, while still retaining the delicacy and refinement that characterize Oriental art in general.

ALL THE TEA IN CHINA

"Spring Rainfall at the Tea Farm" refers to one of China's most venerable institutions: the growing and drinking of tea. The beverage is brewed from the leaves of a shrub with the botanical name of *camellia sinensis*, and the history of tea in China dates back to at least 350 B.C. European explorers introduced tea drinking to the West during the 16th century, and from then on it became increasingly popular. During the 19th century, some of the most beautiful of all sailing ships, the famous clippers, raced each other halfway around the world to bring tea from China to Boston, New York, and London. Meanwhile, European settlers began growing tea in India, Ceylon (Sri Lanka), Malaya, and parts of East Africa.

Above: *An 18th-century Chinese illustration showing workers packing tea at a plantation.*

YUNNAN

Very little is known about composer Wang Xi Lin other than he wrote *Yunnan Scenes* in 1961. This lack of knowledge may be a result of China's Cultural Revolution in the 1960s, when the work of many artists was banned, and the artists themselves were often imprisoned or disappeared. Yunnan *(above)* itself, however, is a province of southwest China, north of Vietnam. It is subtropical in parts, but also mountainous. As well as its tea plantations, Yunnan is rich in minerals such as tin, lead, zinc, and coal.

CHINESE MUSIC

The recorded history of Chinese music goes twice as far back in time as Western music. Some Chinese bronze bells, stone chimes, and clay wind instruments date from around

Below: A modern-day opera performer.

2000 B.C., from about the same period as the Egyptian pyramids.

Chinese philosophers and sages took music very seriously,

Above: *Street performers with traditional instruments.*

relating it to the higher harmonies of the universe, much as Plato and Pythagoras did in ancient Greece. From a more practical point of view, the best-known scales in Chinese music are the pentatonic, or five-note scales, roughly corresponding to the black notes of a piano. Chinese music also employs many stringed and wind instruments, but is noted above all for its percussion: bells, gongs, and wood blocks. The mainstay of Chinese music has always been opera. The old Imperial court opera had more in common with a religious ritual, but there have been many other, more popular forms—traditionally performed by traveling troupes of players, usually at festival times. Much of this ancient tradition lives on in what is today called the Peking Opera.

KEY NOTES

The other descriptive pieces included within Wang Xi Lin's Yunnan Scenes are: "On the Mountain Road," "Evening Song," and "Torch Festival."

CLAUDE DEBUSSY *1862–1918*

Estampes

PAGODES

The "pagodes" (pagodas) of the title are Buddhist temples—tapering structures usually several tiers high. But the real inspiration for this piano piece was Debussy's experience with Indonesian gamelan music during his visit to the Paris World Exhibition of 1889 (for which the Eiffel Tower was built). The soft, delicate chimes and rhythms of this music, with its hints of the Oriental pentatonic, or five-tone, scale, instantly captured his imagination. Years later he magically recreated the exotic and haunting sounds in this, one of his most impressionistic and atmospheric compositions.

DEBUSSY'S ENGRAVINGS

Debussy wrote his set of three piano pieces collectively titled *Estampes* (meaning "Engravings") in 1903. Like "Pagodes," the other two pieces evoke special moods and places. They are the Spanish-inspired "La Soirée dans Grenade" ("Evening in Granada") and the innovative "Jardins sous la pluie" ("Gardens in the Rain").

GAMELAN MUSIC

The gamelan music that entranced Debussy is a speciality of Java and the neighboring Indonesian island of Bali. The word "gamelan" means "struck with a hammer," and although most gamelan ensembles include one or two stringed or wind instruments, they consist mainly of percussion: special kinds of gongs, pots and kettles *(right)*,

chimes, xylophones, and drums. Such music, with its generally soft but hypnotic rhythms and tones, dates back to at least the 1st century A.D. By tradition, each town or village makes its own instruments, so that every gamelan band or orchestra has its own distinctive sound. A large gamelan ensemble may include over eighty percussion instruments of different types.

ORIENTAL SEDUCTION

Debussy is not the only composer to have been captivated by gamelan music. For instance, it inspired Ravel to write "La Vallée des cloches" in his *Miroirs*. Poulenc introduces a passage very much like that of a gamelan orchestra in his *Concerto, for Two Pianos*. And after a visit to the Far East, Britten wrote his ballet *The Prince of the Pagodas (left)*, with its own echoes of gamelan music.

KEY NOTES

Gamelan orchestras include percussion instruments of: "definite pitch," such as xylophones, which sound the pitched notes of a scale; and "indefinite pitch," such as most drums and gongs, which don't produce a precisely pitched note and provide rhythmic patterns and color.

GEORGE GERSHWIN *1898–1937*

Cuban Overture

Like many Americans, Gershwin was greatly attracted to the Old World charm and New World hedonism of Cuba. This overture captures the brash spirit of the Caribbean island as the music plunges straight into the intoxicating rhythm of the rumba. Percussion is provided by claves (two rounded sticks of hardwood tapped sharply together) and maracas (dried gourds with beans or seeds inside to create a rattling effect). A brief clarinet solo introduces a calmer middle section, which is then spiced up by a sudden entry of the strings with a strong, bluesy phrase. The music then winds itself up again for a return of the opening rumba. Chords piled one on top of the other make a thrilling end.

ISLAND OF CUBA

Cuba was discovered by Columbus during his first voyage from Spain in 1492. Its early colonial history saw the arrival of European settlers (largely from Spain),

the annihilation of the native population, and the importation of

African slaves. Cuba remained in Spanish possession until Spain was defeated by the United States in the Spanish-American War of 1898 *(above)*, leading to the island's independence in 1902. The U.S. continued to play a considerable part in Cuba's internal affairs until 1958, when, after a lengthy guerrilla war, communist leader Fidel Castro *(left)* overthrew the regime of Fulgencio Batista.

AMERICA'S PLAYGROUND

Gershwin wrote this piece following a vacation to Cuba in 1932. Because of Cuba's proximity to the U.S. (the island is less than one hundred miles from the southern tip of Florida), it was a tropical playground for wealthy Americans for many years. Casinos flourished in Cuba under American patronage—especially in Havana, the capital. But relations between the countries soured following Castro's communist takeover in 1958.

THE RUMBA

Gershwin's original title for his *Cuban Overture* was *Rumba*. This, the most infectious of all Latin American rhythms, may have originated as a ritual dance in a voodoo cult, with singers uttering incantations against the background of the beat. By the time Gershwin became acquainted with the rumba, it had become one of the most popular ballroom and nightclub dances in the Western world. The Australian-born composer and pianist Arthur Benjamin also wrote a delightful piece in imitation of the rumba, in 1938, although he named this *Jamaican Rumba*.

CUBAN EXPORTS

Cuba has long been famous for its rum and Havana cigars. Rum, the spirit of the Caribbean, is a by-product of the sugarcane plantations *(right)* laid down by early colonists. The name probably comes from "rumbullion," meaning "great tumult"—a good way to describe the bubbling and boiling of the fermenting sugarcane.

Cuban cigars are famed throughout the world for their quality and attractive packaging *(left)*. The secret of a good cigar lies in the quality of the tobacco leaves, which are folded and wrapped whole by hand.

Credits & Acknowledgments

PICTURE CREDITS

Cover /Title and Contents Pages/ IBC:
Getty Images AKG London: (Claude Monet: Cap
d'Antibes in Mistral): 4, 8(t), 25(tl); Archive
Photos: 24(l & br); Catherine Ashmore: 22(b);
Bridgeman Art Library, London/The Fine Art
Society, London (Jean Baptiste Vanmour: A
Turkish Hunting Party): 2; Musée des Beaux-
Arts, Rouen (Felix Ziem: View of Istanbul): 3(tl);
Nordiska Museet, Stockholm (Swedish School:
The Ralambs Paintings): 3(r); Cooley Gallery,
Old Lyme, Connecticut (Norton Bush: Tropics of
North America): 10; Christie's London (Augustin
Brunais: A Linen Market): 11(bl); Victoria &
Albert Museum, London: 18; Bonhams, London:
19(l); Comstock ©1998: 14; Dee Conway: 20(l);
E.T. Archive: 3(bl); Mary Evans Picture Library:
5(tl & b), 7(bl & tl), 11(tl), 12(t & b), 15(tl), 16,
17(tr), 24(tr), 25(bl); Eye Ubiquitous/ Robert
Donaldson: 6; Sue Passmore: 17(l); Getty
Images: 19(r), 21, 23, 25(r); Robert Harding
Picture Library/Richard Ashworth: 9; Hulton
Getty: 7(r); Hutchison Library/John Hatt: 13;
Lebrecht Collection: 5(tr), 8(b), 11(r), 15(bl),
17(br); Chris Stock: 20(r), 22(t); Science &
Society Picture Library: 15(r).

All illustrations and symbols: John See